Pipeline Accident Report

**Natural Gas Pipeline Rupture
and Subsequent Explosion
St. Cloud, Minnesota
December 11, 1998**

NTSB/PAR-00/01
PB2000-916501
Notation 7178A
Adopted July 11, 2000

National Transportation Safety Board
490 L'Enfant Plaza, S.W.
Washington, D.C. 20594

National Transportation Safety Board. *Natural Gas Pipeline Rupture and Subsequent Explosion, St. Cloud, Minnesota, December 11, 1998.* **Pipeline Accident Report NTSB/PAR-00/01. Washington, DC: NTSB, 2000.**

Abstract: About 10:50 a.m. on December 11, 1998, while attempting to install a utility pole support anchor in a city sidewalk in St. Cloud, Minnesota, a communications network installation crew struck and ruptured an underground, 1-inch-diameter, high-pressure plastic gas service pipeline, thereby precipitating a natural gas leak. About 39 minutes later, while utility workers and emergency response personnel were taking preliminary precautions and assessing the situation, an explosion occurred. As a result of the explosion, 4 persons were fatally injured; 1 person was seriously injured; and 10 persons, including 2 firefighters and 1 police officer, received minor injuries. Six buildings were destroyed. Damage assessments estimated property losses at $399,000.

The major safety issues identified in this investigation are the adequacy of the safety and emergency procedures used by Cable Constructors, Inc., crews when working in the vicinity of underground facilities and the adequacy of St. Cloud Fire Department procedures and training for responding to natural gas leaks.

As a result of its investigation of this accident, the Safety Board makes safety recommendations to the Research and Special Programs Administration, the Occupational Safety and Health Administration, the Associated General Contractors of America, the National Utility Contractors Association, the Power and Communications Contractors Association, the National Cable Television Association, the American Public Works Association, and the International Association of Fire Chiefs.

Contents

Executive Summary v

Factual Information 1
   The Accident 1
   Injuries 8
   Damage 8
   Personnel and Training 8
      CCI 8
      Sirti 10
      NSP 11
   Pipeline Operations 12
   Background of Accident 12
   Meteorological Information 13
   Medical and Pathological Information 13
   Survival Aspects 14
      Emergency Response After the Explosion 14
      Disaster Preparedness 16
      Fire Department Procedures and Training 16
      NSP Public Awareness Program 17
   Investigation 17
      Site Description 17
      Gas Monitor Testing 17
      Previous Underground Facility Strikes 18
   Other Information 18
      Events Following the Accident 18

Analysis 20
   Exclusions 20
   The Accident 21
   Contractor Response 22
   Fire Department Response 26
   Excavation Damage Prevention 27
   Excess Flow Valves 29

Findings 31
   Conclusions 31
   Probable Cause 31

Recommendations 32
   New Recommendations 32
   Previously Issued Recommendations
      Classified in this Report 33

Executive Summary

About 10:50 a.m. on December 11, 1998, while attempting to install a utility pole support anchor in a city sidewalk in St. Cloud, Minnesota, a communications network installation crew struck and ruptured an underground, 1-inch-diameter, high-pressure plastic gas service pipeline, thereby precipitating a natural gas leak. About 39 minutes later, while utility workers and emergency response personnel were taking preliminary precautions and assessing the situation, an explosion occurred. As a result of the explosion, 4 persons were fatally injured; 1 person was seriously injured; and 10 persons, including 2 firefighters and 1 police officer, received minor injuries. Six buildings were destroyed. Damage assessments estimated property losses at $399,000.

The National Transportation Safety Board determines that the probable cause of this accident was the lack of adequate procedures by Cable Constructors, Inc., to prevent damage to nearby utilities when its anchor installation crews encountered unusual conditions such as striking an underground obstacle. Contributing to the severity of the accident was the delay by Cable Constructors, Inc., in notifying the proper authorities.

The major safety issues identified in this investigation are the adequacy of the safety and emergency procedures used by Cable Constructors, Inc., crews when working in the vicinity of underground facilities and the adequacy of St. Cloud Fire Department procedures and training for responding to natural gas leaks.

As a result of its investigation of this accident, the Safety Board made safety recommendations to the Research and Special Programs Administration, the Occupational Safety and Health Administration, the Associated General Contractors of America, the National Utility Contractors Association, the Power and Communications Contractors Association, the National Cable Television Association, the American Public Works Association, and the International Association of Fire Chiefs.

Factual Information

The Accident

On December 11, 1998, a crew of four Cable Constructors, Inc., (CCI) workers was tasked with installing a utility pole support anchor[1] vertically through a concrete sidewalk in the city of St. Cloud, Minnesota. (See figure 1.) The anchor (figure 2) was being installed as part of a project by Seren Innovations, Inc., (Seren) to construct a fiber-optic communication system in the St. Cloud area. Sirti Ltd. (Sirti) had been hired to provide all engineering, design, drafting, mapping, licensing, permitting and specification development, and program management for the construction of the system, and CCI had been hired to perform the actual construction work.

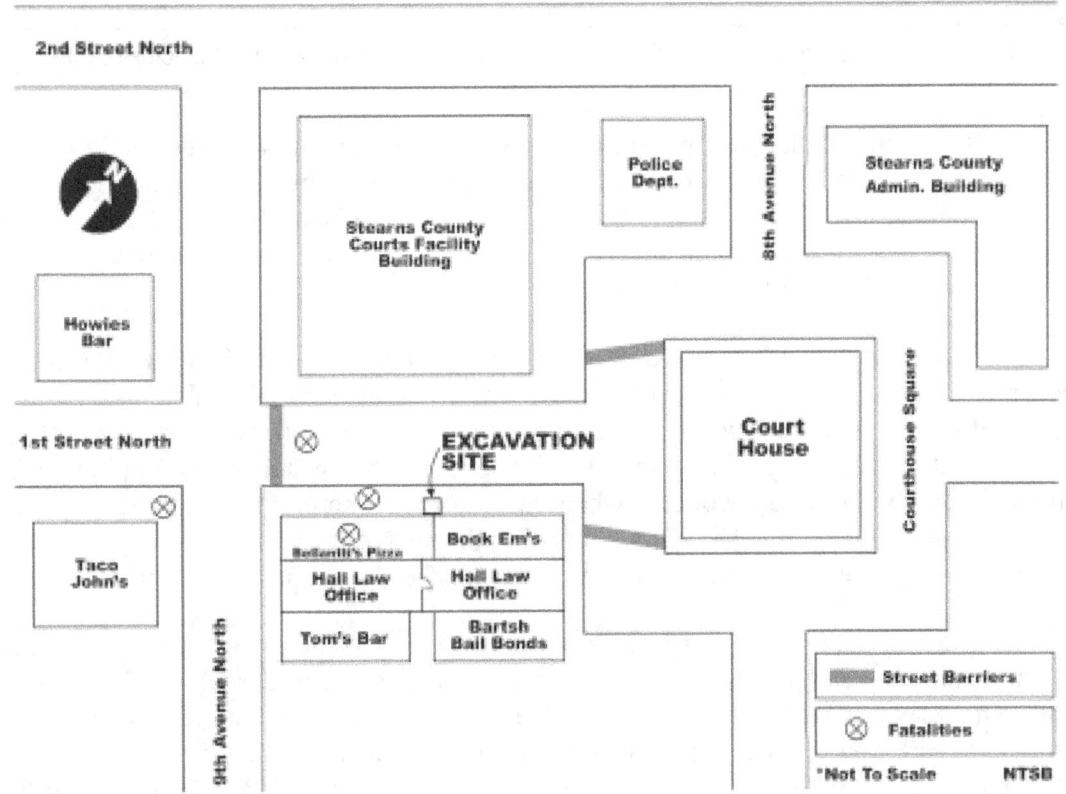

Figure 1. Accident Area

---

[1] The anchor was a steel rod, 5 feet 6 inches long and 3/4 inch in diameter, with a closed-loop eye at the top and a spoon-like helix, cut at an angle, at the bottom. The helix acts as a bit during installation.

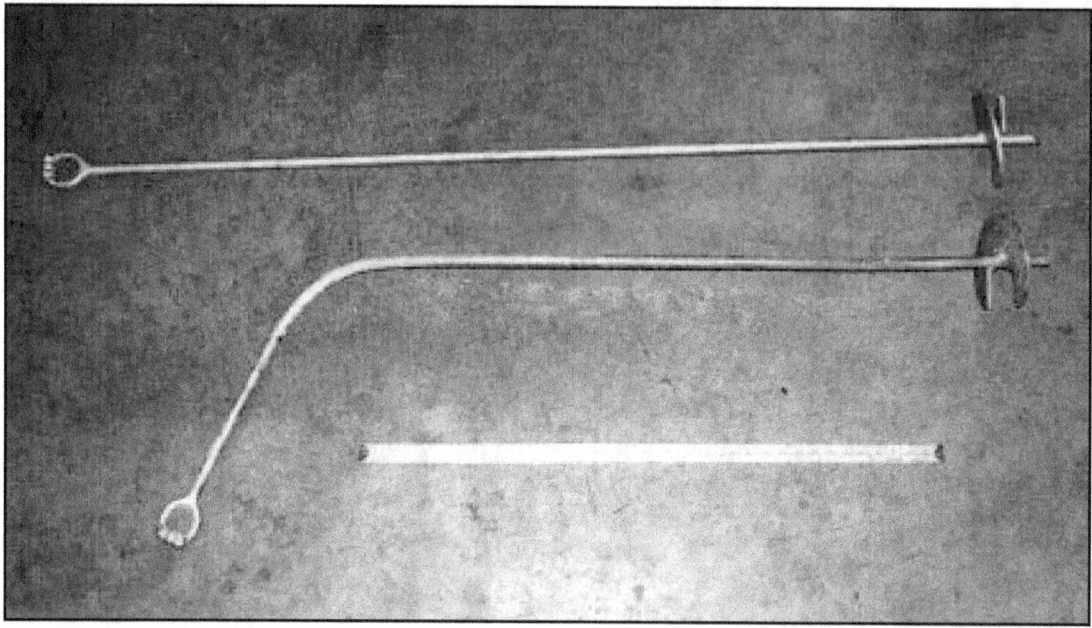

Figure 2. Unused anchor (top) and accident anchor after removal from accident site

Before installation was begun, the crew foreman measured the distance from the planned anchor site to the marked location of a gas pipeline owned by Northern States Power Company (NSP) and used to provide gas service to Book Em's Bar. Because the distance from the marked location of the pipeline to the drill site was more than 2 feet, he determined that the installation of the anchor could proceed.[2]

The workers used a jackhammer to break about a 9-inch-diameter hole in the concrete sidewalk. They then placed an auger known as an "anchor cranker" (a gasoline-powered earth auger that had been specially modified to install anchors) on top of the anchor, and the crew began using the machine to auger the anchor into the ground. (See figure 3.) According to the workers, when the anchor had bored to a depth of 1 1/2 to 2 feet, it hit something hard. The object impeding the anchor's travel was later determined to be a large granite slab about 18 inches wide, 90 inches long, and 8 inches thick.

The crew removed the auger and struck the top of the anchor with a sledgehammer in an attempt to break up what crewmembers thought was a rock or rocks in the anchor's path. The crew then reattached the auger to the anchor, and all four men recommenced the attempt to screw the anchor into the ground. They stated that the anchor then appeared to proceed normally, with no further unusual resistance, and they believed the anchor had broken through the obstacle or been deflected to the side of it. They said that "everything went fine, just as normal" until the top of the anchor was about 12 to 18 inches from the surface. At that point, they noticed dirt blowing out of the anchor hole and immediately

---

[2] The distance from the marked location and the anchor site was later determined to be 38 inches. Had the distance been less than 2 feet, CCI policy and Minnesota State law would have required that the crew expose the utility line before beginning installation of the anchor.

Figure 3. The "anchor cranker" auger used to install the anchor that ruptured the pipeline

began to smell gas. They then stopped the auger and released it. At that point, according to the foreman, "it [the auger] just laid over towards the [utility] pole." (See figure 4.)

After telling other crewmembers to keep people off the street and away from the leaking gas, the crew foreman went into Book Em's Bar with a crewmember to telephone his supervisor. The foreman reached the CCI site project manager about 10:51 a.m.[3] and told him that his crew had struck a gas pipeline while installing an anchor. The foreman later estimated that "no more than a minute" elapsed from the time he smelled gas to the time he made the phone call to his supervisor.

The CCI site project manager told the foreman to follow the company's utility strike procedures, and he went over the procedures with the foreman. The procedures were described in an August 19, 1998, memorandum from Sirti to all CCI supervisors. These procedures were not written into a CCI workplace accident and injury reduction program as required by Minnesota State law. In regard to notification, the procedures stated:

> Any utility strike will require immediate notification of the utility. If gas, immediately extinguish all ignition sources in the immediate vicinity such as motors, smoking, divert all traffic in the area, notify the utility. Isolate the area by barricading to restrict access. It may also be necessary to evacuate the area....

The procedure did not advise supervisors to call 911. The foreman said that after completing the call, he told the four people in the bar of the gas leak outside and informed them that they should not smoke, nor should they exit the building using the doorway near the escaping gas.

---

[3] Unless otherwise noted, times used in this report are based on telephone records or witness statements.

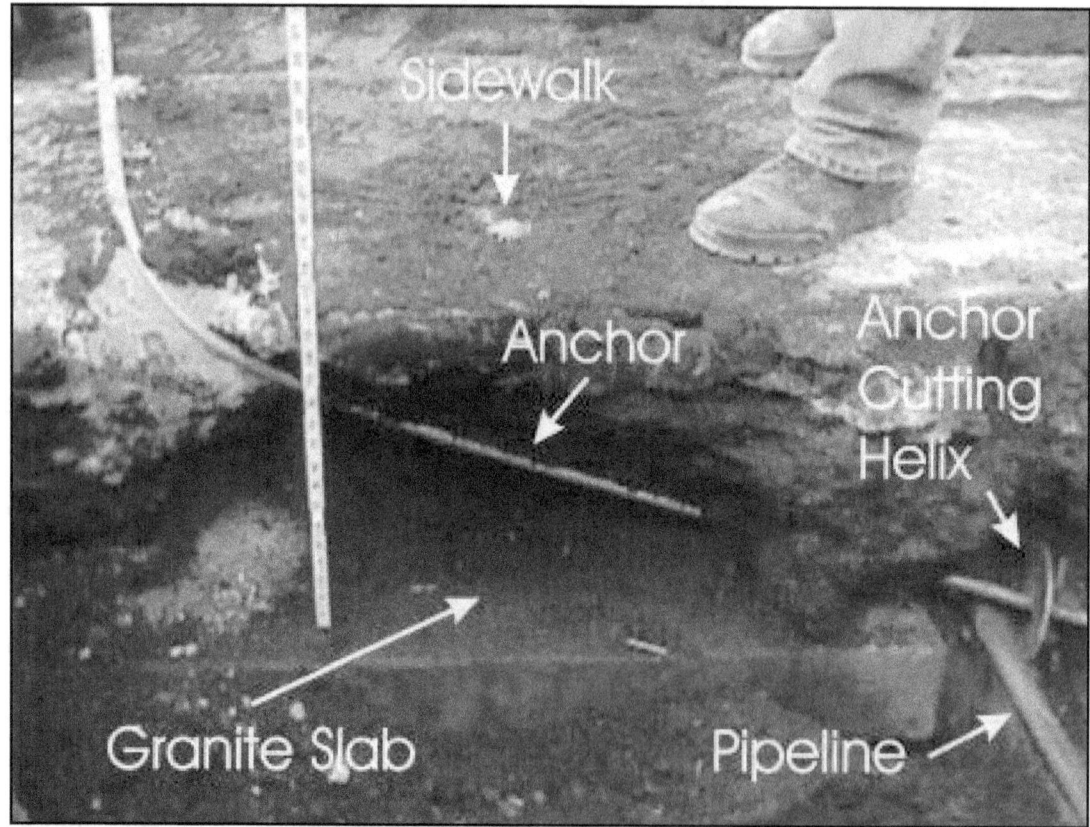

Figure 4. Anchor installation site as revealed by postaccident excavation

The CCI site project manager, as required by Seren's utility damage reporting procedures, then telephoned the Sirti safety coordinator and told him that a gas line had been hit. According to phone records, this call was made about 10:52 a.m. The CCI site project manager said he did not know all of the people to call in St. Cloud. The CCI site project manager said the Sirti safety coordinator told him to call NSP and to let NSP employees make the emergency response calls.

The Sirti safety coordinator told the CCI site project manager that he (the safety coordinator) would immediately leave for the accident site, which he did. On the way, he placed a cell phone call to Seren management, informing them that a gas line had been hit and he was on his way. Some time thereafter, the CCI site project manager departed his office for the accident site. Along the way, he placed a cell phone call to NSP's customer service 800 number to report the leak. According to cell phone records, this call was placed at 11:21 a.m.

Meanwhile, the CCI foreman had gone back to the site to make sure his crewmembers had blocked off the area. He directed that cones and orange tape be used to help keep out vehicular traffic. Minnesota State Law, Chapter 216D.06, required an excavator who damages an underground facility to notify the operator and "take immediate action to protect the public and property and to minimize the hazard until the operator's personnel or emergency responders have arrived." While gas was exiting the ground, a CCI crewmember moved the crew's aerial truck[4] into Courthouse Square and to the north of First Street North. He parked the truck so as to help prevent southbound Courthouse Square traffic from entering First Street North.

After the CCI crew had placed cones and strung orange tape across First Street North where it adjoined Ninth Avenue North, the crew waited for the emergency responders (who, in fact, had not yet been called) and tried to keep people away from the taped off, secured area. The CCI foreman later said,

> For about the first 10 minutes, we had people coming and going, and then people were slowly dissipating. There weren't people coming and going anymore. So basically the street was shut off.

By this time, a receptionist in the Stearns County Administration Building was receiving complaints by telephone and from walk-ins of a strong smell of gas outside. The receptionist relayed the reports downstairs to the office of the Stearns County building facilities director. Upon learning of the reports, the facilities director left by the west entrance of the administration building to investigate. Once outside, he called to have an air handler turned off in the Administration Building.

Knowing of construction on Second Street North, the facilities director approached the site and asked the excavators if they had hit a gas line. The excavators said they had not and pointed him toward the CCI workers. After walking past the police department building and smelling gas, he asked the CCI workers if they had damaged a gas line. The crew foreman told him they had. The director asked if the crew had called the fire department, and the crew foreman reported that they had not. The director then, about 11:05 a.m., placed a cell phone call to the Stearns County chief deputy sheriff and reported the leak. The deputy sheriff then called the sheriff's department dispatcher, who immediately called the St. Cloud Fire Department. At 11:06 a.m., Engine Company 21, based at Fire Station 1, about 2 blocks from the leak site, was dispatched to the scene. According to telephone records, at 11:07 a.m., the fire department dispatcher notified the NSP dispatcher of the leak.

Also about 11:06 a.m., St. Cloud police units 41 and 42 were assigned for traffic control in front of Book Em's Bar because of the gas leak. About the same time, unit 40, a police sergeant, reported that the area had already been barricaded and that police assistance was available to the fire department through the dispatcher.

The firefighters arrived on the scene about 11:08 a.m. According to interviews, a CCI employee moved the tape to allow the engine company into the secured area. The first responders in the engine company included a lieutenant and three firefighters. The lieutenant said he immediately took notice of the wind direction when he arrived at the site. He later said that he planned to use the information to decide which buildings needed to be evacuated first if evacuation became necessary.

---

[4] This truck is known as an aerial truck because it had a lift to allow workers to connect cables to utility poles.

One of the firefighters, accompanied by another firefighter, began testing the area using a hazardous and combustible gas monitor.[5] After radio approval from his lieutenant, and within a minute of arrival, the other firefighter moved the fire truck to the east end of First Street North to eliminate a possible ignition source.

The Sirti safety coordinator said he arrived at the scene about 11:15 a.m. He said he parked across the street from the police station and walked to the accident site. He took several photographs of the anchor location and the general area around the scene.

Four vehicles were parked on First Street North next to Book Em's Bar. The St. Cloud Fire Department lieutenant told the firefighters that NSP would need to bring heavy equipment into the area to repair the leak and that the vehicles would have to be moved. The lieutenant then walked to the police department building and asked that the license numbers for the parked vehicles be researched and their owners contacted. None of the owners were contacted, but they all eventually came out of nearby buildings and moved their vehicles.

With another firefighter at his side, the firefighter with the gas monitor first tested the concentration of natural gas above the leak site. He then performed the same test alongside the buildings housing Book Em's Bar and Bellantti's Pizza and Deli. The firefighter who carried the gas monitor said the area "smelled really bad." He said he essentially got no reading when he placed the monitor directly adjacent to the hole in the ground made by the anchor. He said that the monitor's lower explosive limit (LEL) reading went from -2 to 0.[6] A firefighter stated that they had not had time to do a fresh-air calibration[7] of the monitor because of the short distance between Fire Station 1 and the accident site.

After the fire truck moved to the east end of First Street North, the CCI site project manager arrived on Courthouse Square. He parked his truck on Courthouse Square so as to prevent traffic from entering the east end of First Street North. With the CCI project manager's truck on one side of Courthouse Square and the crewmember's aerial truck on the other side, traffic could not travel from Courthouse Square toward the east end of First Street North.

About 11:16 a.m., two NSP trucks arrived. As was done earlier for the fire department, a CCI lineman moved the tape to permit entry for both NSP trucks. An NSP gas technician specialist arrived in one truck, which he parked on the street alongside the damage area. He then went to the location of the damage to assess its extent and to talk to the CCI foreman. An NSP locator technician (the individual who finds and marks the

---

[5] The hazardous and combustible gas monitor used by the St. Cloud Fire Department was similar to a combustible gas indicator except that it had sensors for both combustible and toxic gases.

[6] *Lower explosive limit* refers to the lowest concentration of a flammable gas that can be ignited. NSP standards state that the LEL of its natural gas is about 4.8 percent. Gas monitors typically indicate the percentage of LEL, meaning that an NSP gas monitor reading of 100 percent would indicate a natural gas concentration of about 4.8 percent.

[7] To ensure accurate readings, the monitor is to be turned on in fresh air, after which it automatically completes a 20-second self-test and start-up sequence.

locations of buried utilities) was in the other truck, which was parked behind the gas technician specialist's truck. With NSP personnel on scene, two of the fire department responders joined the third already at the fire truck, while the lieutenant remained in the vicinity of the leak.

At the anchor leak site, the NSP gas technician specialist asked the CCI foreman to fill out a damage report detailing how the gas line was damaged and providing the address of the responsible contractor. While this report was being filled out, the NSP gas technician specialist was readying his equipment.

Witnesses stated that after the form was completed, the NSP gas technician specialist entered Book Em's Bar at street level (the building did not have a basement). Inside the bar, he took readings on a combustible gas indicator and was overheard stating he obtained a reading of 7 percent.[8] Bar patrons said the gas technician specialist then left the bar to look for an entrance to the basement of the adjacent building, which housed Bellanti's Pizza and Deli. The four persons who were in the bar during this time later told police that no one at any time asked them to evacuate the building.

While the gas technician specialist was taking his readings, according to witness statements, the NSP locator technician was determining if the service line had been properly marked. He was also seen assisting with the movement of a vehicle from the secured area. According to radio and cell phone records, about 11:29 a.m., an explosion occurred in the basement of the building where Bellanti's Pizza was located.

Three firefighters were in their truck at the time of the explosion. They reported that they saw no fire but that they could see little because their vehicle was immediately enveloped in a cloud of dust. Two of the firefighters exited the fire truck while the third used the radio to report the explosion and request ambulance service. He said he "knew that there were injuries." A police officer patrolling nearby also radioed a report of the explosion. After making the report, one of the firefighters then moved the truck to the northeast, putting the county facilities building between the fire truck and the explosion site.

According to NSP, when the NSP gas technician specialist received the call of the leak, about 11:09 a.m., he immediately called for a company construction crew, which was equipped to shut down the damaged portion of the line. At the time of the explosion, this three-person crew was 2 blocks away from the accident site. About 11:30 a.m., the NSP construction crew foreman radioed the NSP dispatcher to report the explosion. The NSP dispatcher directed 26 gas technicians to the explosion site. An NSP manager stated that the technicians were sent to help close off the damaged line and to enter and check all adjacent buildings in the surrounding area for potential gas-related problems. NSP workers stopped the flow of gas to the damaged gas line at 12:25 p.m. and shut off electrical power at 12:31 p.m.

---

[8] Although the gas technician specialist was killed in the explosion and the gas monitor was not recovered, because NSP employees were trained to use their monitors to measure LEL, the 7 percent probably referred to the LEL rather than to the concentration of gas in the air.

According to the report of the Minnesota State fire marshal, the explosion occurred in the basement of the building where Bellanti's Pizza was located. The basement walls were made of stacked stones and crumbling mortar. According to the fire marshal's report, gas collected in the basement of the building and was ignited by an unknown source. In the basement of the building were several potential sources of ignition, including gas water heaters.

Injuries

Table 1. Injuries

Type of Injury[a]	NSP Employees	Emergency Responders	Building Occupants	Other	Total
Fatal	2	0	1	1	**4**
Serious	0	0	1	0	**1**
Minor	0	3	2	5	**10**
Total	**2**	**3**	**4**	**6**	**15**

[a] 49 *Code of Federal Regulations* 830.2 defines fatal injury as "any injury which results in death within 30 days of an accident" and serious injury as "an injury which: (1) requires hospitalization for more than 48 hours, commencing within 7 days from the date the injury was received; (2) results in a fracture of any bone (except simple fractures of fingers, toes, or nose); (3) causes severe hemorrhages, nerve, or tendon damage; (4) involves any internal organ; or (5) involves second or third-degree burns, or any affecting more than 5 percent of the body surface."

Damage

In addition to the building containing Bellantti's Pizza and Deli, the explosion destroyed the buildings containing Book Em's Bar, Tom's Bar, and Bartsh Bail Bonds, and the two buildings containing the Hall Law Offices. The law office buildings were joined with a fire door. The blast also damaged the Stearns County court facilities building and the buildings housing Taco John's and Howies Bar. According to the St. Cloud city assessor, the damage assessment for the buildings destroyed by the natural gas explosion was $399,000. (See figure 5.)

Personnel and Training

CCI

The CCI crew foreman had a total of 14 nonconsecutive years' experience with the company, about half of it as a foreman. He had taken 3 years off the job for personal business and had returned to CCI as a lineman about 3 months before the accident. He said he had received no formal refresher training upon his return. He had been promoted back to foreman about 2 weeks before the accident.

Figure 5. Postaccident aerial view of affected area

One lineman on the crew had been with CCI for 5 1/2 months. Another CCI lineman had about 3 months' experience before the accident. This lineman was a machinist before coming to CCI, and he had no previous communications or cable installation experience. The third lineman on the crew said that he had been working for CCI for only about 2 weeks but that he had 19 months' experience as a lineman before joining CCI.

The CCI site project manager had been working for CCI for 3 years. Before this, he had worked for a cable installation company and as a self-employed cable installer.

CCI conducted initial training for new employees. Much of the initial training was task-related and was focused toward reviewing the work that they would be performing. The initial training also entailed working in the field with experienced individuals who would show new employees the proper way to complete tasks such as pole-climbing and running and overlashing cable.

The initial training covered equipment related to worker safety (hard hats, vests, and cones), but it did not cover what an employee should do in the event of a natural gas pipeline strike. According to meeting records, pipeline strikes were addressed at a special October 23, 1998, meeting held among Seren, NSP, Heath Consultants (utility locating),[9] and CCI. Participants at the meeting included Seren's director of network construction and

---

[9] Utility companies sometimes use utility-locating services rather than their own employees.

operations, CCI's site project manager, and NSP's district operations manager and damage prevention coordinator. Although Sirti was the safety project coordinator, no one from Sirti is listed as attending this meeting. The meeting covered related subjects such as locating underground facilities.

According to the meeting minutes, the meeting was held because "NSP and Seren together decided that we needed a meeting to better control the situation we have with safety as it related to locating gas and electric services, particularly given recent incidents that have occurred." According to officials, a number of incidents had occurred in which yellow-paint locate marks had not been placed directly above the underground facility. Before the meeting, NSP had been contracting out its utility locating to Heath Consultants. As a result of the meeting, NSP assigned two full-time utility locators to the Seren project and put the contract locator under the direct supervision of an NSP locator. To help ensure that locate marks were located directly above underground facilities, the idea of pre-construction "walkouts" was discussed, along with the need for daily meetings at excavation sites between the locator and Seren excavators to pinpoint utility locations. It was determined that improved mapping and map reading would also help ensure that locate marks would be placed directly above underground facilities. During the meeting, the CCI site project manager specified the need for a 24-inch distance between the excavation and the locate marks.

Emergency procedures for Seren contractors were also discussed at the October 23 meeting. The topic discussion started when Seren's director of network construction and operations asked "Once we do have a strike, what is the procedure?" NSP officials then said they would send out a person immediately and that police and fire departments would be needed to keep the crowds away. Later in the meeting, NSP provided attendees with a "tip sheet" containing a step-by-step process in the event an underground natural gas line should be struck during excavation or other construction. The tip sheet advised workers first to shut down all equipment in the immediate area, then "Call 911 and/or radio dispatcher and request that they call 911 to alert the Fire and Police Departments." No tip sheet or written emergency procedures were available at the site of the accident.

CCI construction crews were required to attend "construction" meetings every Wednesday at 10 a.m. According to CCI, at these meetings, workers would discuss incidents that occurred during the previous week. These Sirti-run meetings were also called "safety meetings" because Sirti maintained a log of utility strikes, and the workers would analyze how an incident occurred and how a similar incident could be prevented in the future.

Sirti

The Sirti safety coordinator who responded to the accident had completed a Minnesota Safety Council course entitled "An Introduction to Occupational Safety" in June 1998.

NSP

The NSP gas technician specialist initially sent to check the leak was killed in the explosion. Company records show that the technician had completed the company's "Gas Emergency Training" course in February 1998 and had completed the final course test with no errors.

The locator technician who responded to the leak was also killed. He had taken the gas emergency training course in February 1995 and had passed the final test. He had also taken a course entitled "Recognizing Emergency Conditions" in August 1995. He was not required to take the training course annually because he was not a gas operations employee and therefore would not respond to a gas leak in the same capacity as a gas technician. Because NSP is also the provider of electric power for St. Cloud, the locator technician would locate both electric and gas underground facilities. He had been the individual who had marked the location of the pipeline before the anchor installation was begun, and he went to the site to verify that he had properly marked the pipeline's location.

According to NSP officials, the company offered a number of courses designed to prepare NSP employees to respond to gas emergencies. The officials stated that the training has a special section on outside leak emergencies and that a considerable part of this section is about leak classification guidelines. Leak classifications involve the volume, location, area, system pressure, concentration, duration, and spread rate of a leak. Company representatives said employees were taught that a leak classification involves the possible migration of the gas and the proximity of a leak to a building foundation. The gas emergency training course lesson plans state that experience is imperative in evaluating a leak and assigning repair priority and that experience is needed to recognize where gas may be migrating.

In addition to the above training, NSP's St. Cloud office gas operations employees were required to attend a half-day fire school during the summer and 90-minute safety meetings each month. These meetings covered 17 planned subjects such as carbon monoxide safety, heat stress, and winter safety. An NSP training officer stated that the safety meetings were less structured or planned than the company's training courses. None of the safety meetings specifically covered the procedures needed in the event of an underground gas leak next to a building.

The NSP Gas Safety Training Department required that new gas operations employees go through a formal apprenticeship program. On an ongoing basis, all gas operations employees are required to take a first-aid course every 3 years and 11 different courses annually. Required courses included confined space work, excavation and shoring, and gas emergency training.

Pipeline Operations

NSP completed the original installation of the gas service line serving Book Em's Bar on October 29, 1982. The polyethylene main and service pipelines were installed for use at 7 inches water column pressure (approximately 1/4 psig). According to the company, NSP planned to possibly upgrade the system later to high pressure, and the pipelines were tested to 100 psig after installation. An excess flow valve (EFV) was not required by regulation and was not installed.

Records show that the service pipeline and meter set to Book Em's Bar were "uprated" to high pressure on August 19, 1998. No excavation was done to uprate the pipeline. The service pipeline meter set was changed to fit a high-pressure, 60 psig system, and the service pipeline was again tested to 100 psig. After August 19, 1998, and at the time of the accident, the pipeline operating pressure at the outlet of the regulator station was about 60 psig.

Background of Accident

On March 10, 1998, a contract was completed between Seren, a fully owned subsidiary of NSP, and Sirti. The contract stipulated that Sirti would provide all engineering, design, drafting, mapping, licensing, permitting, and specification development for the construction of a two-way fiber-optic telecommunications system throughout the St. Cloud area.

On July 15, 1998, Seren authorized Sirti to provide the construction project management services for the St. Cloud telecommunications system. As project manager, Sirti would coordinate all construction and testing activities and administer all contractor's documents. Contract correspondence between Seren and Sirti indicated that Sirti would hire a safety manager who would prepare a safety manual and be responsible for enforcing all Federal and State regulations.

On August 5, 1998, Seren signed a contract with CCI to construct the telecommunications system throughout the St. Cloud area. Although Sirti was already chosen to be the project and safety manager, the contract between Seren and CCI had no mention of Sirti. CCI officials were aware that Sirti was the project manager, and CCI subleased office and warehouse space from Sirti. CCI started field construction under this contract on August 10, 1998.

On December 8, 1998, after using the Gopher State One-Call system, CCI's aerial construction manager met with eight underground facility operators,[10] including NSP, and informed them of the locations where CCI planned to install utility-pole support anchors.

---

[10] The underground facility operators included the city of St. Cloud, the city of Waite Park, TCI Cablevision, the State of Minnesota Department of Transportation, Norstan Communications, NSP, Seren, and U.S. West (telephone).

The facility operators marked their facilities in these areas. CCI planned to do the work at these sites between December 8 and December 11. The One-Call ticket was for 21 locations.

Meteorological Information

According to weather data recorded at the St. Cloud airport, at the time of the accident, the skies were clear and the wind was blowing out of the southwest at 8 mph. Climatological data for the city of St. Cloud indicate that the weather for a month before the accident was unseasonably mild, with the average temperature being 10.7° F warmer than normally recorded for that time of year. Had it not been for the unseasonably warm weather, CCI would have had to postpone the anchor installations because of frozen ground.

Medical and Pathological Information

Four people were fatally injured in the accident, including the NSP gas technician and the NSP locator. Also killed were a pedestrian walking outside the taped-off area and a tenant of one of the rented rooms above Bellantti's Pizza. The tenant was found in the basement of the collapsed building with debris beneath and over his body. Cause of death in each case was multiple traumatic injuries due to natural gas explosion.

Eleven people, including two firefighters and one police officer, were injured. An employee of the law offices, one of four trapped persons extricated from the rear of the law offices building, sustained serious injuries from falling debris. The remaining 10 people received minor injuries, including abrasions, lacerations, and inhalation injuries. They were treated at St. Cloud Hospital and released.

U.S. Department of Transportation (DOT) rules for postaccident alcohol and drug testing (49 *Code of Federal Regulations* (CFR) 199.3 and 11(b)) do not cover workers such as CCI employees at the scene of the gas explosion or those involved in the excavation activities that preceded the accident. Covered employees are those persons who perform operating, maintenance, or emergency response functions regulated by 49 CFR Parts 192, 193, or 195.

After discussions with NSP and Seren, CCI, about 10 hours after the accident, directed five involved employees to St. Cloud Hospital for the collection of specimens. The five employees included the crew, the crew foreman, and the project manager, who was the first member of management to be notified of the leak. Arrangements were made for MedTox Laboratories, Inc., in St. Paul, Minnesota,[11] to collect the specimens and

---

[11] MedTox Laboratories, Inc., was on a U.S. Department of Health and Human Services list of laboratories meeting minimum standards to perform urine drug testing.

perform the tests. According to the times indicated on the MedTox laboratory sheets for the blood and urine test reports, the earliest specimen collection was 9:35 a.m. on the day of the accident, and the last collection was 10 a.m. the next day.[12] The other collections were recorded as taking place between 10:30 p.m. and 11:20 p.m. on December 11. The MedTox test results for alcohol in blood were positive at or above 0.02 g/dl for one employee. For another employee, marijuana metabolite was present in urine at or above the 15 ng/ml level.

The Safety Board asked the crewmembers about their activities between the time of the accident and the time their specimens were collected. They said they returned to the shop for their paychecks. On the way home, they went together to a bar and had "several" drinks. The foreman said that he drank a "couple" more beers when he got home. Everyone on the crew said that they had not consumed alcohol or used drugs within 8 hours of reporting for work on the morning of the accident.

The specimens remaining after the MedTox tests were shipped to the Civil Aeromedical Institute (CAMI) for additional testing at the request of the Safety Board. The CAMI tests revealed the presence of alcohol and marijuana in the specimens of two of those tested.

According to CCI officials, after the accident, the company began requiring preemployment drug screening and conducting random drug testing of its employees.

Survival Aspects

Emergency Response After the Explosion

Immediately after the explosion, one engine company each responded from St. Cloud Fire Department's Fire Stations 2 and 3, and a ladder truck responded from Fire Station 1. Fire department personnel notified Gold Cross Ambulance Service to respond and requested heavy excavation equipment. Crewmembers of Engine Company 21, already on scene, began search and rescue operations immediately.

Four people were trapped inside the rear portion of the Hall law offices, which was between the Bellantti's building and Tom's Bar. Three of those trapped were extricated by firefighters within 20 minutes. Some 30 minutes after that, the fourth person was freed and taken to the hospital. None of these individuals reported seeing any NSP or fire department personnel before the explosion.

At 11:30 a.m., St. Cloud Police Department Unit 43 advised the Stearns County Sheriff's Department dispatcher of the explosion. All available ambulances were asked to

---

[12] MedTox forms for one employee show the time of urine collection as 9:35 a m. on December 11, which was about 2 hours before the explosion. The time shown for collection of a blood specimen for the same employee was 10 a m. on December 12, the day following the accident. The Safety Board asked for but did not receive information from MedTox that would explain these discrepancies.

respond to the scene, as were all available law enforcement personnel. A request was also made for construction equipment.

About the same time, the St. Cloud fire chief and the assistant fire chief, who was the incident commander, arrived on scene. At 11:31 a.m., the St. Cloud Police Department began evacuating the immediate area, including Courthouse Square and the north side of the courthouse building. At this time, all of the St. Cloud off-duty firefighters and volunteer division firefighters were called to report to duty. At 11:32 a.m., a command post was established 100 feet west of the intersection of Ninth Avenue North and First Street North and a staging area was established at the rear of Fire Station 1. Also about 11:32 a.m., Engine 21 firefighters notified the incident commander that they were going to begin evacuation of the Stearns County courts facilities building. At 11:33 a.m., the incident commander requested additional NSP personnel because of the gas leak and downed electrical wires. The first ambulance arrived at 11:34 a.m.

At 11:37 a.m., the fire chief activated the St. Cloud *Emergency Action Plan*. At 11:38 a.m., the fire chief asked for help from the Waite Park and Sauk Rapids fire departments.

At 11:42 a.m., the St. Cloud police established an evacuation perimeter. This perimeter included the Law Enforcement Center, the courthouse, and the Stearns County Administration Building.

At 11:44 a.m., Gold Cross Ambulance Service called the St. Cloud Hospital and informed the emergency trauma center charge nurse of the gas explosion and advised her that approximately 20 patients possibly could be transported to the hospital. Subsequently, the hospital evaluated its resources and determined that three air ambulances were available to transport patients to burn centers if necessary.

By 11:47 a.m., all injured survivors, with the exception of the seriously injured and trapped victim, had been removed from the immediate area surrounding the explosion. The evacuation perimeter was further secured using police line tape and road barricades with security checkpoints established.

At 11:50 a.m., the owner of the building housing Bellantti's Pizza informed a police supervisor that two rooms on the second floor of the Bellantti's building were rented. At 12:07 p.m., the incident commander called for the Anoka County Search and Rescue Canine unit.

At 12:09 p.m., St. Cloud Hospital initiated its disaster plan and notified 50 medical professionals to respond to an upper floor staging area. The emergency trauma center monitored the activities of the ambulance crews on site and was kept informed on the conditions of patients and their transportation to the hospital. A total of 11 people were either transported by ambulance or arrived by private vehicle at the hospital. At 1:30 p.m., the hospital's disaster plan was discontinued.

At 1:51 p.m., the Anoka County Search and Rescue Canine Unit arrived on scene. At 2:24 p.m., St. Cloud police received reports that two individuals had been in a rented room above Bellantti's at the time of the explosion. At 3 p.m., the police department confirmed that all four people who had been inside Book Em's Bar at the time of the explosion had been accounted for. At 3:05 p.m., police officers were assigned to start door-to-door checks within the affected area. At the same time, Red Cross workers were on site at a nearby home for senior citizens to assist with a possible evacuation.

Search and rescue operations continued with the use of manual and heavy equipment until approximately 10 p.m., in the event that more victims were buried in the debris; however, none were found. At 10 p.m., the St. Cloud Police Department and the 34th Military Police Company of the Minnesota National Guard secured the area for the night. NSP continued operations in the area, restoring power and gas service to the senior citizens home and to other buildings in the area.

Disaster Preparedness

The city of St. Cloud implemented its disaster plan for the accident. The purpose of the basic plan was to ensure the effective, coordinated use of the resources available to the city so as to: (1) maximize the protection of life and property; (2) ensure the continuity of government; (3) sustain survivors; and (4) repair essential facilities and utilities. Prior to the accident, the most recent certification of the plan by local authorities was September 9, 1998.

The last full-scale disaster drill conducted by the city of St. Cloud before the accident was on May 21, 1998. The drill simulated an airplane accident at St. Cloud airport. According to hospital officials, St. Cloud Hospital routinely performs two internal disaster drills annually.

Fire Department Procedures and Training

Although all of the fire department responders were trained on the basic characteristics of natural gas, at the time of the accident, the St. Cloud Fire Department had no written procedures in place providing detailed guidance on responding to natural gas leaks. The firefighters were instructed during in-house training, State-sponsored training, and training sponsored by NSP to be aware of wind direction as well as the general characteristics of natural gas. The American Gas Association's (AGA's) pamphlet *A Guide to Controlling Natural Gas in Emergencies* was also reviewed and distributed by NSP. Prepared by the AGA as a guide to firefighters, the pamphlet provides a brief overview of natural gas and its characteristics. In a section dealing with steps to take when gas is escaping outside a building, the pamphlet recommends:

> If unignited gas is escaping from the ground, from an excavation or from an open pipe outside a building - **NOTIFY THE GAS COMPANY IMMEDIATELY**. A safe area surrounding the location should be cleared, roped or barricaded. Extinguish all open flames. Prohibit smoking. Check surrounding buildings, cellars in particular, for any presence of gas odors. Restrict or reroute all traffic until gas company personnel can bring the gas flow under control.

This pamphlet outlined the actions to take in the event of an underground gas leak next to a building.

NSP trains its employees that gas can migrate underground. As a part of its public awareness program (see next section), NSP provides information and instructional classes to fire departments on the hazards of natural gas. Before the accident, the most recent training class regarding natural gas had been provided to the St. Cloud Fire Department in October 1995.

NSP Public Awareness Program

According to company officials, NSP has a public awareness plan for the safety of the public and contractors working in and around natural gas. The plan covers excavation safety, and the information is communicated through radio, television, and newspaper ads, in addition to billing inserts. All forms of communication emphasize the need to call Gopher State One-Call before excavating. Some forms of communication, especially newspaper ads and billing inserts, include whom to call for carbon monoxide problems, gas leaks, or incidents when the odor of natural gas is detected. The ads and inserts state that in the case of a suspected gas leak, a person should evacuate a building, should not turn on any light switches, and should call NSP from outside the building. Excavation safety includes working with various groups such as the Gopher State One-Call, the Metropolitan Utility Coordinating Committee, the Minnesota Utility Contractors Association, and other groups to prevent excavation damage.

Investigation

Site Description

Postaccident Safety Board investigation revealed a yellow paint mark on the sidewalk in direct line with two other yellow paint marks, one over and perpendicular to the curb and another on the sidewalk closer to Book Em's. The paint marks ran in a straight line toward a gas riser located inches from the Book Em's building wall. Each of the paint marks was about 2 feet long and was directly over the gas service pipeline.

Gas Monitor Testing

Four days after the accident, with fire department and Safety Board personnel present, the gas monitor readings that were obtained by firefighters at the accident scene before the accident were downloaded from the memory device within the monitor, and the monitor was calibrated. The calibration of the monitor was tested by exposing the unit to a calibration gas with a concentration that was 50 percent of LEL. When tested against this gas, the monitor registered 34 percent of LEL. Also, the timing mechanism on the monitor was in error by about 4 minutes.

Previous Underground Facility Strikes

Although the gas line location in this accident was accurately marked, during the investigation, the Sirti safety manager stated that an NSP locating contractor had done a poor locating job in the past. Sirti submitted to the Safety Board a list of 37 previous underground facility strikes, with several attributed to improperly located or unmarked underground facilities.

NSP records showed that as a result of excavator error, CCI and its subcontractor had previously damaged NSP natural gas pipelines, including incidents on October 7 and 30, 1998. CCI had also damaged NSP's underground electrical facilities and the underground facilities of others. About 1 year before this accident, CCI had struck a telephone cable and was cited and fined by the Minnesota Office of Pipeline Safety.

According to NSP, while Seren contractors had been installing telecommunications in the St. Cloud geographic area, they had damaged underground natural gas facilities in 15 locations (including the accident location) over a 4-month period. In about half of the incidents listed, damage was attributed to improper locating.

Seren subcontractors other than CCI had also damaged NSP natural gas pipelines. On December 2, 1998, a Seren contractor damaged a gas main. The St. Cloud Fire Department responded and NSP had to bypass the leak to avoid disrupting service to about 100 customers.

Other Information

Events Following the Accident

After the accident, the Minnesota Occupational Safety and Health Administration (MNOSHA) cited CCI for not having a written plan to avoid damage to the underground gas lines in and near the construction area and for not having a complete workplace accident and injury reduction (AWAIR) program. The CCI program did not list methods to identify, analyze, and control existing hazards. MNOSHA also cited Sirti and Seren for not having a complete AWAIR program.

Following the accident, Seren replaced CCI as a contractor for the project. The new contractor was removed after it too was involved in damaging underground facilities. To prevent further incidents, the companies involved and local authorities jointly decided that all future Seren contractors would be required to undergo training with NSP. Additionally, NSP would have a safety inspector at each site when anchors were being installed.

As part of its postaccident activities, the St. Cloud Fire Department developed, in conjunction with NSP, standard operating guidelines for responding to natural gas emergencies. The guidelines state that gas can migrate underground into buildings, that gas monitors should be used both outside and inside buildings to check for the concentration of gas, that ignition sources should be eliminated and buildings ventilated, and that people in the vicinity should be evacuated to a safe area. The department has also revised its standard operating procedures to direct that firefighters (1) not rely exclusively on gas monitors to detect gas concentrations, (2) eliminate possible sources of ignition until the leak is stopped, (3) evacuate people and maintain site security, and (4) detect possible underground migration by checking buildings, manholes, and confined spaces in the affected area. The procedures note that "it can take several hours for the Gas Company to shut off gas in a large high-pressure pipeline."

In a June 5, 2000, letter to the Safety Board, the St. Cloud Fire Department outlined steps it had taken to ensure the proper calibration of its gas monitors and noted that NSP had provided the department with three gas monitors that NSP calibrates and maintains.

Since the accident, the city of St. Cloud has adopted a right-of-way management ordinance and hired a specialist to manage the ordinance. The ordinance requires people working in an area designated as having critical facilities (high-risk areas) to submit a gas safety plan with all their permit applications. The ordinance imposes certain requirements for work in these areas depending on the nature of the work and the risks involved. The city, in conjunction with industry representatives, has mapped all the critical facility areas.

After the accident, CCI established a new safety and health program patterned after the Minnesota State AWAIR program. The company hired a full-time safety manager. CCI had all company project managers attend a 10-hour construction awareness class. CCI also reported to the Safety Board that it has enhanced its employee training. CCI now has procedures in place that require 911 to be called immediately in the event a gas line is ruptured.

Effective August 1, 1999, the State of Minnesota revised Minnesota Statute 216D to require any excavator who breaches a pipeline containing hazardous gas or liquid to immediately notify 911. The law states, in part:

> If any damage occurs to an underground facility or its protective covering, the excavator shall notify the operator promptly. When the operator receives a damage notice, the operator shall promptly dispatch personnel to the damage area to investigate. If the damage results in the escape of any flammable, toxic, or corrosive gas or liquid or endangers life, health, or property, the excavator responsible shall immediately notify the operator and the 911 public safety answering point...and take immediate action to protect the public and property.

The director of the Minnesota Division of Emergency Management told Safety Board investigators that State 911 emergency call centers had recorded no noticeable increase in calls to 911 since enactment of the law and that, in the opinion of the official, the law has ensured more timely notification of authorities after excavation damage.

Analysis

The explosion in the St. Cloud accident occurred in the building housing Bellanti's Pizza and Deli. The escaping natural gas from the damaged pipeline apparently migrated underground, through the crumbling foundation of the building, and into the basement. There, exposed to several potential sources of ignition, it exploded.

Because of the delay in notifying the gas company and emergency response personnel, about 18 minutes elapsed from the time the pipeline was ruptured until the first firefighters arrived (about 21 minutes before the explosion). About 26 minutes after the rupture (about 13 minutes before the explosion), gas company personnel arrived. An NSP gas technician specialist was assessing the hazard when the explosion occurred.

The major safety issues identified in this investigation are the adequacy of the safety and emergency procedures used by CCI crews when working in the vicinity of underground facilities and the adequacy of St. Cloud Fire Department procedures and training for responding to natural gas leaks.

The remainder of this analysis addresses factors that were eliminated as causal or contributory to this accident, followed by a discussion of the major safety issues.

Exclusions

NSP marked the location of a nearby gas service line before the CCI construction crew began installing the utility pole anchor through the sidewalk next to the building housing Book-Em's Bar and Bellanti's Pizza. Postaccident excavations confirmed the accuracy of the paint marks that indicated the location of the natural gas line. The Safety Board concludes that the marked location of the ruptured gas line was accurate and was therefore not a factor in this accident.

The CCI crew knew immediately that they had struck and ruptured a gas line when they saw dirt blowing back around the anchor and smelled gas, and they took actions consistent with procedures established by the company. The foreman promptly notified CCI management of the leak, and the crew began restricting public vehicle access to the area.

Toxicological testing of blood and urine specimens revealed that alcohol or marijuana, or both, was present in some of the involved employees; however, the specimens were collected after the employees had returned to their homes for the evening, and the testing could not determine how much alcohol was ingested or when the alcohol and marijuana had been used.

No one reported observing any actions that could be construed as indicating impairment on the part of individuals in the crew who tested positive for alcohol or marijuana while those employees were working on the morning of the accident. Moreover, the crew's collective actions after the leak showed prompt and full compliance with CCI procedures, as well as with the instructions given to the foreman on the telephone by the project manager. The Safety Board therefore concludes that while toxicological testing performed after this accident was not useful for determining whether alcohol or drugs had any influence on the performance of the CCI crewmembers while they were installing the anchor, the crewmembers' actions before and after the rupture indicate that they were likely not impaired by alcohol or drugs at the time of the accident.

The Accident

Installation of the anchor was begun some 38 inches from the marked location of the underground gas line. This distance was 14 inches beyond the 2-foot margin provided for in CCI procedures and Minnesota State law to allow for a possible error in the marking of the location of the gas line. But while this 38-inch distance appeared to be adequate to ensure a safe installation, the length of the anchor was about 66 inches. At this length, the anchor could easily span the distance from the entry point to the pipeline if it were installed at an angle rather than vertically.

The CCI crew stated that they intended to install the anchor vertically, and no evidence was found to indicate that the anchor did not enter the ground vertically. But when the anchor struck the buried granite slab, the crewmembers followed their customary practice and struck the top of the anchor with a hammer until they perceived that the anchor had broken through the obstacle or had deflected off to its side. As the investigation later determined, the anchor had not broken through but had bent and deflected. The anchor apparently continued to bend as the four men applied pressure to the anchor cranker in their attempt to complete the installation. The investigation determined and postaccident excavation revealed that the anchor bent and followed along the upper surface of the buried granite slab until the cutting helix on the anchor tip dropped off the end of the slab, thus striking and rupturing the pipeline.

CCI procedures for protecting underground utilities did not address the risks associated with abnormal conditions underground that could render normal precautions inadequate. The Safety Board found no evidence that anchor installation crews were made aware that even if installation is begun at a safe distance from a buried utility, safety can be compromised if the anchor is allowed to assume an angled path underground. Such a deflection could endanger an underground utility and present a risk to the public. The Safety Board concludes that CCI's anchor installation procedures were inadequate in that they did not address steps to take under unusual circumstances (such as striking a significant underground obstacle) to ensure that buried utilities were protected during the entire installation process, including the underground portion.

In its investigation of a July 21, 1997, accident in Indianapolis, Indiana,[13] the Safety Board found that adequate controls were not in place to prevent an underground pipeline from being damaged during directional drilling, even though indications above ground were that an adequate safety margin was being observed. In the view of the Safety Board, excavation procedures are inadequate if they do not account for the possibility that unusual conditions could negate otherwise effective attempts to protect buried utilities. The Safety Board therefore believes that the Associated General Contractors of America, the National Utility Contractors Association, the Power and Communications Contractors Association, the National Cable Television Association, and the American Public Works Association should advise their memberships to review and revise their anchor installation procedures as necessary to ensure that safety margins around buried utilities are absolutely observed not only above ground but throughout the installation process.

Contractor Response

Within 1 minute of striking the gas line, the CCI crew foreman, following the procedures his company had established for such an emergency, informed his supervisor of the incident. But the supervisor did not immediately notify emergency response agencies. Instead, he called the Sirti safety coordinator, telling him that he did not know whom to call. The safety coordinator told him to call NSP and let NSP employees notify emergency response agencies. The Sirti safety coordinator then departed for the scene. Along the way, he called Seren management to inform them of the leak.

By this time, then, several operational and management levels of the involved companies knew of the leak, yet no one had notified emergency response agencies. In fact, about 15 minutes elapsed before another individual, not associated with the construction project, notified emergency responders. The CCI supervisor did eventually call the owner of the gas line but not until about 30 minutes after the line was struck. By this time, two NSP employees were already on the scene, the company having been notified by the fire department dispatcher.

Had either the crew foreman or his supervisor immediately called 911, responders could have been on the scene within minutes. For example, a fire department vehicle and four firefighters were on the scene within about 2 minutes of being notified, but because of the delayed notification, they arrived some 18 minutes after the rupture and about 21 minutes before the explosion.

Once on scene, the gas technician specialist determined by meter reading that the gas concentration in Book-Em's Bar, at 7 percent of LEL, was some 93 percent below the minimum concentration necessary for an explosion to occur. Because of the proximity of the leak to the bar, this level could have been the result of gas entry through the door of the building. According to witness statements, the gas technician specialist left the bar to find

---

[13] National Transportation Safety Board. 1999. *Excavation Damage to 20-inch-diameter Buried Steel Transmission Pipeline, Indianapolis, Indiana, July 21, 1997.* Pipeline Accident Brief. Washington, D.C.

the entrance to the basement of the building next door. Before he arrived there, however, the explosion occurred, and he was killed. With an earlier start to evaluating the risk of the situation, the gas technician specialist may have been able to determine that gas was, in fact, accumulating in the basement of the Bellanti's building. The gas company and emergency responders may then have decided to evacuate everyone from nearby buildings and out of the area. Additional steps may have been taken to eliminate ignition sources and ventilate the basement. In such an event, the explosion may have been prevented or, at a minimum, some of the people at risk could have been removed from the area.

The Safety Board concludes that had the crew foreman or his supervisor called 911 or the utility owner immediately after the rupture, emergency responders and NSP personnel may have had time to fully assess the risk and to take actions that could have helped either to prevent the explosion or to avoid the resulting loss of life.

In 1997, the Safety Board published a safety study that discussed industry and government actions to prevent excavation damage.[14] The study formalized recommendations aimed at further advancing improvements in excavation damage prevention programs. One area given prominence was emergency procedures applicable when a utility is damaged during excavation. The safety study noted that while Federal regulations require pipeline operators to establish written emergency procedures, the regulations do not apply to excavators, even though "these are the very people that often have responsibility for first response at an excavation disaster." The study concluded that, at a minimum, "excavators should formulate an emergency response plan appropriate for the specific construction site and ensure that employees working at that site know the correct action to take if a buried facility is damaged." The Safety Board therefore made the following safety recommendation to the American Public Works Association (APWA):

P-97-30

Develop guidelines and materials that address initial emergency actions by excavators when buried facilities are damaged and then distribute this information to all one-call notification centers.

The APWA responded on January 26, 1998, stating that the organization would like to meet with the Safety Board to discuss the APWA's ability to implement the safety recommendations in the package that contained P-97-30. The Board replied on March 12, 1998, placing the recommendations in an "Open—Await Response" status pending the outcome of a meeting. A meeting was held on March 12, 1998, and the APWA agreed to look at the package of recommendations and advise the Board regarding which of the actions the APWA could accomplish. The APWA failed to respond further, and the Safety Board, in a June 7, 2000, letter, asked the APWA to provide information about its efforts to implement the safety recommendations. Safety Recommendation P-97-30 remains classified "Open—Await Response."

---

[14] National Transportation Safety Board. 1997. *Protecting Public Safety Through Excavation Damage Prevention.* Safety Study NTSB/SS-97/01. Washington, DC.

The safety study also referenced Safety Recommendation P-95-25, issued to the APWA as a result of the Safety Board's investigation of a 1993 accident in St. Paul, Minnesota:

P-95-25

Urge your members to call 911 immediately, in addition to calling the gas company, if a natural gas line has been severed.

Safety Recommendation P-95-25 has been classified "Closed—Acceptable Action" based on the fact that the APWA revised its *Public Works Practices Manual* to include a chapter on utility coordination that addresses this recommendation.

Common Ground: The Study of One–Call Systems and Damage Prevention,[15] published in August 1999, provides guidance for saving valuable time in emergency notification should a natural gas line be damaged during excavation. The "best practice" regarding contact names and numbers states that

The excavator's designated competent person at each job site has access to the names and phone numbers of all facility owner/operator contacts and the one-call center.

In the St. Cloud accident, no one at the site had contact names and numbers. Not even the CCI site project manager had such a list; he told the Sirti safety coordinator that he did not know whom to call to report the leak.

The "best practice" statement for notification of emergency personnel is as follows:

If the protective coating of an electrical line is penetrated or gases or liquids are escaping from a broken line which endangers life, health or property, the excavator immediately contacts local emergency personnel or calls '911' to report the damage location.

The National Utility Locating Contractors Association (NULCA) has developed guidelines for excavation practices and procedures for damage prevention. The NULCA guidelines, which were revised in September 1997, include a suggested procedure whereby excavators call 911 if excavation damage "involves a potential risk to life, health or significant property damage."

Both the *Common Ground* best practice and the NULCA guidelines suggest that a call to 911 be made only after an excavator determines that excavation damage has occurred that presents a hazard. Minnesota State law, on the other hand, requires that

---

[15] The *Common Ground* report was prepared by more than 160 individuals representing a wide range of interests, organizations, and viewpoints on preventing damage to underground facilities. The project was initiated by the DOT's Office of Pipeline Safety, an element of the Research and Special Programs Administration, in response to the Transportation Equity Act for the 21st Century, Public Law 105-78, signed into law June 9, 1998. The purpose of the year-long study was to identify and validate existing best practices performed in connection with preventing damage to underground facilities.

contractors notify 911 in the event of damage to buried utilities if the damage results in the escape of any flammable, toxic, or corrosive gas or liquid *or* endangers life, health, or property. The wording of the Minnesota law relieves excavators of the responsibility of determining whether damage represents a hazard before they call 911 and the utility owner. The Safety Board prefers this approach to that of the *Common Ground* best practice or the NULCA guidelines.

In the view of the Safety Board, the utility owner and 911 or other appropriate emergency notification number should be called any time a hazardous substance is released from a pipeline through construction damage, regardless of whether those on the scene perceive an immediate danger to public safety. Excavators are not all knowledgeable about what constitutes a hazardous situation. For example, they may not be familiar with the hazards of gas migrating underground, or they may not realize that a pulled pipeline could be broken in more than one place. Emergency responders can usually arrive at the scene quickly and are often trained and equipped to assess such hazards and take appropriate safety measures.

Strengthened requirements to notify utility owners immediately in the event of any damage to a pipeline can also increase safety. The sooner the experts from the operator are notified, the sooner they can apply their knowledge to reduce the public safety risks. Whereas some contractors may previously have waited until the end of the day to report damage to pipelines that did not appear to present an obvious threat, requiring immediate notification of operators could possibly help them prevent a minor problem from developing into a major hazard. Some damage may not result in an immediate leak but may represent a hazard in the future. The pipeline operator can determine if corrective measures are needed to prevent a future failure. If an immediate pipeline leak does occur, the utility owner is in the best position to be aware of the hazards associated with the product in its pipelines and the appropriate safety countermeasures, and to be able to shorten the time until a leak can be stopped.

Additionally, in the Safety Board's view, strengthening the notification requirement will increase awareness on the part of contractors and other excavators of the importance of taking care not to damage utilities, and a reduction in the number of such incidents may be expected.

To help ensure that this issue is addressed on a nationwide basis, the Safety Board believes that the Occupational Safety and Health Administration (OSHA) at the Federal level should require excavators to notify the pipeline operator immediately if their work damages a pipeline and to call 911 or other local emergency response number immediately if the damage results in a release of natural gas or other hazardous substance or potentially endangers life, health, or property.

In the meantime, until OSHA can act on this recommendation, the Safety Board believes that the Path Forward initiative (discussed below in the "Excavation Damage Prevention" section) should promote the immediate notification of the utility owner and emergency agencies whenever excavation damage to a utility results in a release of natural gas or other hazardous substance or otherwise presents a threat to public safety. Because the DOT's Research and Special Programs Administration (RSPA) was instrumental in the creation of the Path Forward initiative, that agency should, through the mechanism of Path Forward initiative, take the lead in promulgating an industry "best practice" that advises excavators to notify the pipeline operator immediately if their work damages a pipeline and to call 911 or other local emergency response number immediately if the damage results in a release of natural gas or other hazardous substance or potentially endangers life, health, or property.

To further raise awareness of the early notification issue, the Safety Board believes the Association of General Contractors, the National Utility Contractors Association, the Power and Communications Contractors Association, and the National Cable Television Association should publicize the circumstances of this accident to their memberships to make them aware of the dangers of damage to an underground utility and the need to immediately call 911 or other appropriate local emergency response number when a natural gas leak or other hazardous condition occurs and to immediately notify utility companies when an underground facility has been damaged.

Fire Department Response

An engine company with a lieutenant and three firefighters arrived within minutes of fire department notification. Firefighters attempted to take gas concentration readings with a gas monitor, but the monitor had not been calibrated in fresh air and gave invalid or unreliable readings. Firefighters continued to attempt readings with the improperly calibrated instrument, all the while working in an environment in which they described the gas smell as "pretty bad." At no point did firefighters check buildings near the leak site to determine if natural gas was accumulating or to help assess the need for a possible evacuation, even though the gas line was continuing to release gas that could migrate through the ground and into nearby buildings, where it could present a danger of explosion. Two of the firefighters near the leak site returned to their truck as soon as two gas company employees arrived. It should have been obvious to the firefighters that a threat continued to exist and that the situation could worsen.

The Safety Board therefore concludes that firefighters of the St. Cloud Fire Department responded quickly to the scene of the leak; however, once on the scene, the firefighters' actions did not fully address the risk to people and property posed by the leak or reduce the consequences of a possible fire or explosion.

As part of its postaccident activities, the St. Cloud Fire Department developed guidelines for natural gas emergency response that address the issues identified in this accident. According to fire department officials, revisions to procedures have been developed that should help prevent a similar accident in the future in the St. Cloud Fire Department's response area. In the view of the Safety Board, all first responders should be prepared to respond effectively to a gas leak hazard.

Timely, effective response to a natural gas emergency can save lives. In an October 30, 1998, accident in Chicago, Illinois, excavation work damaged a 24-inch-diameter natural gas main.[16] The natural gas ignited about 40 minutes later, causing major fire and heat damage to a nearby 15-story high-rise apartment building. Responding fire and police personnel completely evacuated the high-rise building before the gas ignited, with the result that no one was injured in the accident.

The Safety Board believes that the International Association of Fire Chiefs should publicize the circumstances of the St. Cloud, Minnesota, accident to their membership to make them aware of the potential dangers of gas migrating into buildings from damaged underground gas lines. The Safety Board further believes that the association should advise its membership of the need to determine the hazards posed by natural gas leaks and the value of having an evacuation plan in place to be used when the situation warrants.

Excavation Damage Prevention

The Safety Board has long been concerned about the numbers of accidents attributable to excavation damage. In May 1997, the Safety Board added excavation damage prevention to its "Most Wanted" list of safety improvements.[17] Data maintained by RSPA indicate that damage from outside force is the leading cause of leaks and ruptures to pipeline systems, accounting for more than 40 percent of reported failures. Investigation of the St. Cloud accident alone revealed a high incidence of excavation damage to utilities, by different contractors, both before and after the accident.

A 1994 workshop sponsored jointly by the Safety Board and RSPA brought together about 400 people representing pipeline operators, excavators, trade associations, and local, State, and Federal government agencies to identify and recommend ways to improve prevention programs. The Safety Board's 1997 safety study was initiated to analyze the findings of the 1994 workshop, to discuss industry and government actions undertaken since the workshop, and to make recommendations to further reduce excavation damage accidents.

The safety study addressed employee qualifications and training, which has been an issue in a number of excavation-caused pipeline accidents. To address training and qualifications of those not covered by Federal regulations, the Safety Board, on January 6, 1998, issued the following safety recommendation to the APWA:

---

[16] Illinois Commerce Commission, September 1999, *Report of the ICC Staff: Incident at 1507 North Claybourn Avenue, Chicago, Illinois, October 30, 1998.*

[17] In October 1990, the Safety Board developed the "Most Wanted" list, drawn up from previously issued safety recommendations, to bring special emphasis to the safety issues the Board deems most critical. The Most Wanted list is updated as needed.

P-97-29

Review existing training programs and materials related to excavation damage prevention and develop guidelines and materials for distribution to one-call notification centers.

This recommendation has the same history as Safety Recommendation P-97-30, discussed earlier, and is classified "Open—Await Response."

The safety study noted the progress that had been made since 1994 by RSPA and the industry in the area of improving excavation damage prevention programs. But the study concluded that despite improvements in State excavation damage prevention programs, additional efforts were needed to uniformly develop and implement programs that are most effective. On January 6, 1998, the Safety Board therefore addressed Safety Recommendation P-97-15 to RSPA and P-97-25 to APWA asking that the two organizations work in conjunction to:

P-97-15 and -25

Initiate and periodically conduct...detailed and comprehensive reviews and evaluations of existing State excavation damage prevention programs and recommend changes and improvements, where warranted, such as full participation, administrative enforcement of the program, pre-marking requirements, and training requirements for all personnel involved in excavation activity.

Based on an October 30, 1998, RSPA response to Safety Recommendation P-97-15 and on a meeting of representatives from RSPA and the Safety Board to discuss ongoing actions to address the intent of the recommendation, Safety Recommendation P-97-15 was classified "Open—Acceptable Response" on June 29, 1999.

In an April 24, 2000, letter to the Safety Board, RSPA responded in general terms to 29 Safety Board recommendations, including P-97-15. The letter outlined the agency's efforts to create a "self-sustaining private sector non-profit organization" that would "provide an effective forum for information sharing among all stakeholders in damage prevention." These efforts, known as the "Damage Prevention: Path Forward" initiative,[18] are intended to continue the efforts begun with the *Common Ground* study and to address the issues involved in preventing outside force damage to the underground infrastructure. Working committees having been established to direct the formal establishment of the Path Forward program. The Safety Board is encouraged by the promise of the Path Forward program and will follow the development of the program with interest. The classification for P-97-15 will remain "Open—Acceptable Response" pending further action by RSPA.

The Board is also disappointed by the lack of response from the APWA to Safety Recommendation P-97-25. That recommendation has followed the same history as Safety

---

[18] A new nonprofit organization, the Common Ground Alliance, is being formed to continue the Path Forward initiative.

Recommendations P-97-29 and -30, discussed earlier, and remains classified "Open—Await Response."

Excess Flow Valves

Excess flow valves (EFVs) are available that respond to an excessive flow of gas by automatically closing and restricting the gas flow. EFVs therefore can greatly reduce the consequences of service line ruptures.

The Safety Board initially advocated using EFVs on service lines to schools and other buildings in which large numbers of people gather. Later, because EFVs became cheaper and more available, the Safety Board began advocating the installation of EFVs on new or renewed residential service lines. During the 1980s, RSPA, which has oversight responsibilities over the pipeline industry, failed to require EFVs. Consequently, the Safety Board included the use of EFVs on its 1990 list of Most Wanted safety improvements.

On September 26, 1990, as a result of its investigation of five natural gas accidents in the Kansas City-Topeka area, the Safety Board recommended that RSPA:

P-90-12

Require the installation of excess flow valves on new and renewed single-family, residential high pressure service lines which have operating conditions compatible with the rated performance parameters of at least one model of commercially available excess flow valve.

On April 4, 1995, RSPA notified Congress by letter that it had decided not to require universal installation of EFVs and instead would issue performance standards and customer-notification requirements for EFVs. In a September 28, 1995, letter to RSPA, the Safety Board expressed its disappointment with this decision. The Board noted the continued strong evidence that a way was needed to quickly restrict the flow of gas to a failed pipe segment. On September 28, 1995, as a result of RSPA's failure to issue EFV requirements, the Safety Board classified Safety Recommendation P-90-12 "Closed—Unacceptable Action."

On March 6, 1996, as a result of its investigation of a June 9, 1994, natural gas explosion in Allentown, Pennsylvania, the Safety Board wrote to the governors of all 50 States and to the mayor of the District of Columbia asking that they require gas distribution operators to install EFVs in all new or replaced gas service lines when operating conditions are compatible with commercially available valves (Safety Recommendation P-96-3). Of the States that replied, most advised that they intended to follow the lead of RSPA and had no plans to require the installation of EFVs. The State of Minnesota did not respond to Safety Recommendation P-96-3.

Also on March 6, 1996, the Safety Board recommended that RSPA:

P-96-2

Require gas distribution operators to notify all customers of the availability of excess flow valves; any customer to be served by a new or renewed service line with operating parameters that are compatible with any commercially available excess flow valve should be notified; an operator should not refuse to notify a customer because of the customer's classification or the diameter or operating pressure of the service line.

On February 3, 1998, RSPA issued its final rule regarding EFVs. The rule requires gas distribution operators either to install EFVs on new or replaced single-residence service lines expected to operate continuously at not less than 10 psig or to inform customers of the availability and benefits of EFVs and install them if the customer agrees to pay for their installation and maintenance.

On October 6, 1998, the Safety Board classified this recommendation "Closed—Unacceptable Action," in part because the RSPA rule limits required notifications by gas operators to residential customers. As in the case in the St. Cloud accident, many commercial service lines have operating characteristics compatible with the same EFVs that will be installed in residential service lines.

According to an American Gas Association survey, since the issuance of the RSPA final rule on EFVs, approximately one-half of the operators of gas distribution systems have elected to install EFVs, and one-half have developed procedures to inform customers of their availability. NSP's current policy, put in place after the St. Cloud accident, is to install EFVs on all new or replaced service lines that fit the operating requirements of its approved EFVs, regardless of whether the customer is residential or commercial.

Because no further action can reasonably be expected to be taken either by RSPA or the States, the Safety Board, on May 3, 2000, removed the recommendations regarding EFVs from its Most Wanted list. In a July 5, 2000, letter to the Governor of Minnesota, the Safety Board asked for information about Minnesota's intentions with respect to Safety Recommendation P-96-3. Until Minnesota responds to the Safety Board's latest request for information, Safety Recommendation P-96-3 to the State of Minnesota will be classified "Open—Unacceptable Action."

When NSP converted the gas service line from low pressure to high pressure, the line itself was not replaced; therefore, the most recent Safety Board recommendations regarding EFVs would not have applied to this service line. Nonetheless, the Safety Board is convinced of the usefulness of EFVs in preventing pipeline accidents and concludes that had the gas line in this accident been equipped with an EFV, the valve may have closed after the pipeline ruptured and the explosion may not have occurred.

Findings

Conclusions

1. The marked location of the ruptured gas line was accurate and was therefore not a factor in this accident.

2. While the toxicological testing performed after this accident was not useful for determining whether alcohol or drugs had any influence on the performance of the Cable Constructors, Inc., crewmembers while they were installing the anchor, the crewmembers' actions before and after the rupture indicate that they were likely not impaired by alcohol or drugs at the time of the accident.

3. Cable Constructors, Inc.'s anchor installation procedures were inadequate in that they did not address steps to take under unusual circumstances (such as striking a significant underground obstacle) to ensure that buried utilities were protected during the entire installation process, including the underground portion.

4. Had the crew foreman or his supervisor called 911 or the utility owner immediately after the rupture, emergency responders and Northern States Power personnel may have had time to fully assess the risk and to take actions that could have helped either to prevent the explosion or to avoid the resulting loss of life.

5. Firefighters of the St. Cloud Fire Department responded quickly to the scene of the leak; however, once on the scene, the firefighters' actions did not fully address the risk to people and property posed by the leak or reduce the consequences of a possible fire or explosion.

6. Had the gas line in this accident been equipped with an excess flow valve, the valve may have closed after the pipeline ruptured and the explosion may not have occurred.

Probable Cause

The National Transportation Safety Board determines that the probable cause of this accident was the lack of adequate procedures by Cable Constructors, Inc., to prevent damage to nearby utilities when its anchor installation crews encountered unusual conditions such as striking an underground obstacle. Contributing to the severity of the accident was the delay by Cable Constructors, Inc., in notifying the proper authorities.

Recommendations

New Recommendations

As a result of its investigation, the National Transportation Safety Board makes the following safety recommendations:

To the Research and Special Programs Administration:

Through the mechanism of the Path Forward initiative, take the lead in promulgating an industry "best practice" that advises excavators to notify the pipeline operator immediately if their work damages a pipeline and to call 911 or other local emergency response number immediately if the damage results in a release of natural gas or other hazardous substance or potentially endangers life, health, or property. (P-00-1)

To the Occupational Safety and Health Administration:

Require excavators to notify the pipeline operator immediately if their work damages a pipeline and to call 911 or other local emergency response number immediately if the damage results in a release of natural gas or other hazardous substance or potentially endangers life, health, or property. (P-00-2)

To the Associated General Contractors of America: (P-00-3 and -4)

To the National Utility Contractors Association: (P-00-5 and -6)

To the Power and Communications Contractors Association: (P-00-7 and -8)

To the American Public Works Association: (P-00-9 and -10)

To the National Cable Television Association: (P-00-11 and -12)

Inform your membership of the circumstances surrounding the December 11, 1998, accident in St. Cloud, Minnesota, to make them aware of the dangers of damage to an underground utility and the need to immediately call 911 or other appropriate local emergency response number when a natural gas leak or other hazardous condition occurs and to immediately notify utility companies when an underground facility has been damaged.

Advise your membership to review and revise their anchor installation procedures as necessary to ensure that safety margins around buried utilities are absolutely observed not only above ground but throughout the installation process.

To the International Association of Fire Chiefs:

Inform your membership of the circumstances surrounding the December 11, 1998, accident in St. Cloud, Minnesota, to make them aware of the potential dangers of gas migrating into buildings from damaged underground gas lines. Advise your membership of the need to determine the hazards posed by natural gas leaks and the value of having an evacuation plan in place to be used when the situation warrants. (P-00-13)

Previously Issued Recommendations Classified in this Report

The following previously issued safety recommendations are classified in this report:

To the Research and Special Programs Administration:

Initiate and periodically conduct, in conjunction with the American Public Works Association, detailed and comprehensive reviews and evaluations of existing State excavation damage prevention programs and recommend changes and improvements, where warranted, such as full participation, administrative enforcement of the program, pre-marking requirements, and training requirements for all personnel involved in excavation activity. (P-97-15)

Safety Recommendation P-97-15 (previously classified "Open—Acceptable Response") is again classified "Open—Acceptable Response" in the "Excavation Damage Prevention" section of this report.

To the State of Minnesota:

Require gas distribution operators to install excess flow valves in all new or renewed gas service lines, when operating conditions are compatible with commercially available valves, including service lines supplying schools, churches, and other places of public assembly. (P-96-3)

Safety Recommendation P-96-3 (previously classified "Open—Await Response") is classified "Open—Unacceptable Action" in the "Excess Flow Valves" section of this report.

BY THE NATIONAL TRANSPORTATION SAFETY BOARD

JAMES E. HALL
Chairman

JOHN A. HAMMERSCHMIDT
Member

JOHN J. GOGLIA
Member

GEORGE W. BLACK, JR.
Member

CAROL J. CARMODY
Member

Adopted: July 11, 2000